MARTIAL ART

Brendan Kennelly was born in 1936 in Ballylongford, Co. Kerry; and was educated at St Ita's College, Tarbert, Co. Kerry, and at Trinity College, Dublin, where he has been Professor of Modern Literature since 1973. He has published more than 30 books of poems, including six volumes of selected poems, most recently *A Time for Voices: Selected Poems 1960-1990* (Bloodaxe, 1990) and *Breathing Spaces: Early Poems* (Bloodaxe, 1992). His latest books are *The Man Made of Rain* (Bloodaxe, 1998), written after he survived major heart surgery (also available on cassette), two new collections, *Begin* (Bloodaxe, 1999) and *Glimpses* (Bloodaxe, 2001), and *Martial Art* (Bloodaxe, 2003), versions of the Roman poet Martial.

He is best-known for two controversial poetry books, *Cromwell*, published in Ireland in 1983 and in Britain by Bloodaxe in 1987, and his epic poem *The Book of Judas*, (Bloodaxe, 1991), which topped the Irish bestsellers list: a shorter version was published by Bloodaxe in 2002 as *The Little Book of Judas*. His third epic, *Poetry My Arse* (Bloodaxe, 1995), did much to outdo these in notoriety.

His translations of Irish poetry are available in *Love of Ireland: Poems from the Irish* (Mercier Press, 1989). He has edited several anthologies, including *The Penguin Book of Irish Verse* (1970; 2nd edition 1981), *Between Innocence and Peace: Favourite Poems of Ireland* (Mercier Press, 1993), *Ireland's Women: Writings Past and Present*, with Katie Donovan and A. Norman Jeffares (Gill & Macmillan, 1994), and *Dublines*, with Katie Donovan (Bloodaxe Books, 1995). He has published two novels, *The Crooked Cross* (1963) and *The Florentines* (1967).

He is also a celebrated dramatist whose plays include versions of *Antigone* (Peacock Theatre, Dublin, 1986; Bloodaxe, 1996); *Medea*, premièred in the Dublin Theatre Festival in 1988, toured in England in 1989 by the Medea Theatre Company, and broadcast by BBC Radio 3 and published by Bloodaxe in 1991; *The Trojan Women* (Peacock Theatre & Bloodaxe, 1993); and Lorca's *Blood Wedding* (Northern Stage, Newcastle & Bloodaxe, 1996).

His *Journey into Joy: Selected Prose*, edited by Åke Persson, was published by Bloodaxe in 1994, along with *Dark Fathers into Light*, a critical anthology on his work edited by Richard Pine. Åke Persson has also published *That Fellow with the Fabulous Smile: A Tribute to Brendan Kennelly* (Bloodaxe, 1996).

His cassette recordings include *The Man Made of Rain* (Bloodaxe, 1998) and *The Poetry Quartets: 4*, shared with Paul Durcan, Michael Longley and Medbh McGuckian (The British Council / Bloodaxe Books, 1999).

BRENDAN KENNELLY

MARTIAL ART

BLOODAXE BOOKS

1 85224 621 9   paperback edition

First published 2003 by
Bloodaxe Books Ltd,
Highgreen,
Tarset,
Northumberland NE48 1RP.

www.bloodaxebooks.com
For further information about Bloodaxe titles
please visit our website or write to
the above address for a catalogue.

Bloodaxe Books Ltd acknowledges
the financial assistance of Arts Council England.

Cover printing by J. Thomson Colour Printers Ltd, Glasgow.

Printed in Great Britain by
Cromwell Press Ltd, Trowbridge, Wiltshire.

for Jim Farrelly

MARTIAL

Marcus Valerius Martialis was born in Bilbilis, Spain, about the year 40 A.D. He went to Rome when he was 25 or so, stayed there for some 35 years, then returned to Bilbilis where he died about the year 104.

In Rome, he met the writers Lucan, Seneca and Quintilian, who may have introduced him to wealthy influential patrons. Such connections probably helped him to escape starvation. He went on to become friendly with other leading writers such as Juvenal, Quintilian, Pliny the Younger, Silius Italicus, Stella, Valerius Flaccus.

After proving himself a sharp, often acerbic observer of life in Rome, and having recorded his observations in epigrams, Martial, having spent most of his life in that packed, bustling, expensive city, decided to return to his birthplace. For a while, he enjoyed life back in Bilbilis, but soon grew bored of the congested spite of small-town life. After about four years there, he died.

MARTIAL ART

Translation is a relationship in which, like most relationships, one staggers and steadies oneself, finds and loses, is lost and found in ways that constitute rhythm. The challenge is not just to live *with* that rhythm, but to live it.

This relationship is between two writers, two languages, and two times in time. Martial lived two thousand years ago. Today, he's alive and kicking, spotting and chopping, praising and satirising. He revels in his own contrasts and contradictions. He's a Spaniard in Rome, a wandering provincial in a confident metropolis, a proud, vigilant loner, a bit of a beggar at times, seeming to desire what he castigates, to give away what he cherishes. He is a satirist trying to define generosity, happiness and love. But always, always, he is candid and clear. Candour and clarity in brief, punchy poems. Martial's gifts, given in the generous, mischievous Martial way. If he'd been a boxer, he'd have developed a new kind of knockout punch, smiling at his victim as he walked back to his corner.

When I think of Martial, I don't find myself saying 'had' or 'was'. I say 'has' and 'is'. He *is*. He *has*. Now and forever.

His brief poems inspire brief poems. There are verses here which I wrote after trying to translate him, or while I tried to translate him. I include them because they wouldn't have existed without the unique animation of the Martial spirit. He generates new life, new pictures, new words. You could sing him at times.

His themes are many and varied. He writes of money, food, wine, furniture, style, power, sex, corruption, love, hatred, streets, darkness, families, poverty, snobbery, poets, poetry, polished deceit, aesthetic backstabbers, High Art, low artists, metropolitan egotism and arrogance, politics, escape to the countryside, property, law, education, greed, manipulative men and women, cliques, loners, talkers and chatterboxes of every shade and notive, patrons, misery, the happy life, clothes, enemies, gossip, friends, flattery and the old, constant problem of personal survival and hope of self-renewal.

That's Rome two thousand years ago. That's Dublin today. London and New York and Paris too, for all I know. Martial knows. He never quits sniffing human realities. He looks for, and finds words that tell the smell. He tells it well.

Latin and English seem to dance with each other, such is the energy generated by the old classical language, and the readiness to expand and experiment, to play, pun and act with the energy inherent in English, in Englishes. What is called translation is a bridge linking these energies. A translation is born in a state of wonder at the potential of both languages; and the translator's aim should be, I believe, to produce as good a poem as possible in English. This may involve omission, amplification, even moments of distortion, but as one walks the bridge from Latin to English, there is frequently a strange sense of being led by words which demand that you make your choices and get on with the journey. This journey from language to language, from comprehension to choice, is the real adventure, involving winning and losing, of translation. It's a kind of gamble, a continuing risk, backwarding and forwarding of relationship, intense work that is also a fascinating game. Is one translating Martial? Or is Martial, smiling and mischievous as ever, translating the translator?

There is frequently the sense that hidden, multiple meanings lurk in these precise, voluptuous Latin words, and also that eager clusters of English words are waiting to play the game. The bridge of meaning is also a bridge of sound and fun. Words leap and fly across centuries.

As with the two languages, so with the two times in time. Allowing for the possibility that one is caged, perhaps without realising it, in one's contemporary world, I was amazed at the similarities in Martial's verse between Rome two thousand years ago and Dublin today. Huge differences, of course, but also astounding similarities. That bridge again. How much of "progress" is a kind of self-deception about the nature of our journey across the bridge?

I believe that Martial is a true *homo ludens*. No matter how savage his satire, his direct abuse, his scurrilous candour, he is ultimately a playful and, I would say, a compassionate genius with a determination to know his own mind, to communicate that mind's contents to other people and, always aware of his own limitations, to enjoy and spread the kind of rich laughter that springs from recognising and admitting his own various forms of poverty. I see a sharp, strolling, threadbare (at times), visionary man, knowing the world about him, in touch with the world within himself, at once bewildered, attentive and articulate, and ready to smile while he says what he has to say as clearly and candidly as he can while leaving it to readers to make of his verses what they will. I hope I've captured a fair glimpse of him.

BRENDAN KENNELLY

Three things

Three things make an epigram sing:
brevity, honey, sting.

How it is

Some of my poems are good, some
not up to scratch, some
bad.

That's how it is with most books,
if the truth were told.

Who tells the truth about truth, my dear?
Make way for the judge and the jester.

Reminder

A good poem reminds me
of a certain kind of thrilling crime
a few know how to commit.

That's how it is in Rome today,
and will be in the Glen of the Larks
in two thousand years time.

A long road

When you meet me, Meenus, you say
'May I send my boy for a copy of your Epigrams?'
No need to trouble the lad, Meenus.
It's a long road to the Pear Tree
and I live up three steep flights of stairs.
You can get what you want nearer home.
There's a shop close to Caesar's Forum
where you'll find the works of the poets,
mine among them.
The shopkeeper will sell you a Martial
for ten pounds.

'You're not worth that much,' I hear you say.

Right you are, Meenus, right you are.
How many pounds will buy a star?

Nothing

You say my epigrams are too long.
Yours are shorter.
You write nothing.

Brevity

This writer of couplets is bent on brevity.
What's the good of brevity
if his couplets fill a book?

Praise

Smootus says my book is uneven.
I see this as praise of my work.
A bad book is fat with unvarying quality.

Your own

You're a fair-minded man, Cecil.
I've noticed this on a few occasions.
If I read you some of my couplets
you immediately quote Catullus or Marsus.
Do you wish to compliment me,
as if you were quoting something inferior,
so that the contrast is praise of my verse?
I suppose so. In future, however,
I'd rather you quoted your own.

Martial law (more or) less

If a picture is stolen
        and nobody misses it
                and the thief loves it

                let him keep it.

Not long

A poem is not long
if it contains nothing you can cut
without lessening its life.

All

Some candid lines are all I have to give.
Words ask only one thing of me: my life.

I Hear

I hear Cinna has written some verses against me.

A man is no writer
if his poems have no reader.

Pleasure

What's the point of writing things, Sextus,
which few people begin to understand?
Your books need a clever, interpreting god,
not an ordinary reader. You think
Cinna a better writer than Virgil.
On the basis of such thinking, may your works
receive equal praise. As for myself, Sextus,
I hope my verse gives pleasure to critics,
provided it gives pleasure to other people
without the help of such insightful souls.

His own

Paulus buys poems, recites them
as if he'd written them.
What a man buys
he calls his own
in certain parts of town.

Rud

It is rumoured, Rud, that you recite
my poems in public
as though you'd written them.
I'll send you a book of my poems for nothing
if you agree they should be heard as mine.
Should you wish them to be heard as yours,
buy them, Rud. They're mine no longer.

A reading

Dear Rud, the book from which you are
giving a reading is mine
but since you read so badly
it's yours.

What I love

You never know.
Neither do I.
That's what I love about philosophy.
Fill, O Sophie, goddess of wisdom,
        my empty head
with the living wisdom of the dead.

She's back

The goddess of corpses is back in town
wearing a cool, conquering gown.
Who's her next man?

Stress

The god of divination is under stress.
What he'll say
is anyone's guess.

I want you, Loftus

I run from your table, Loftus,
splendid and all as it is, rich
with the choicest food and drink.
When you recite, you ruin it all.
I don't want you to set before me
turbot, mullet, salmon or trout.
I don't want your mushrooms or your oysters.
I want you, Loftus, to keep your mouth shut.

Wrappers

Dear Loftus, unless you change your boring poems
into wrappers for trout and salmon
you'll be known as the man
who dined and died on his own.

Remedy

You complain of a sore throat, Molarus.
The remedy is simple.
Don't talk at all.

Muffler

Why do you wrap that muffler around your neck
when you're going to recite poems to us visitors?
The muffler is better suited to our ears.

Enchantment

Some voices are most enchanting
when they're not heard.
Their silence is purest music.

Such men are we

Yes, I'm a poor man, Callistratus,
but I've a certain fame. My poems
are read throughout the world. People say
'That's Martial'. Life brings to me
what death brings to certain men.
A hundred pillars support the roof of your mansion.
Your coffers are choked with gold.
You are Lord of the Land in Egypt.
You own countless flocks of sheep in Parma.
I am poor. You are rich. Such men are we,
but what I am you can never be,
while anyone in any crowd anywhere
can be what you are.

No hurry

When Virgil lived, Rome read Ennius.
Homer was scorned in his own time.
Only Corinna recognised her Ovid.

     Be in no hurry, my little books.
Recognition will come, doesn't matter how late.
Glory is slow and certain. I can wait.
I thrive on envy, suck skill from hate.

Less

To avoid humiliation, anxiety, nightmare,
become the bosom friend of no one.
You'll have less pleasure, less pain.

Forever

The only wealth that is yours forever
is the wealth you give away.

Transience

Beware of simply amusing people.
You'll be transient as a chuckle.

The reason

You ask me why I like the country air.
I never meet you there.

Wasisdoesdid

He was a doctor. Now he's an undertaker.
He does as an undertaker what he did as a doctor.

Doctor's visit

I wasn't well. You came quickly, Symmachus,
with a hundred students whose freezing hands
felt my pulse. I wasn't feverish before, Symmachus.
        I am now.

A little vision

We went to the baths together, dined together,
next morning he was found dead. Why?
He dreamed he saw Doctor Hermocrates.
A little vision may prompt a man to die.

Three goats

This case is not about assault, murder, poison,
arson, blackmail, war, or selling one's soul.
        It is about my three goats
which my loving neighbour stole.
Your eloquence flows convincingly.
Only remember, my three goats matter to me.

Proof

Segius says there are no gods, no heaven.
The proof he offers? He's a rich man.

Itself

You are not a vicious man, Zoilus.
You are vice itself.

Request

Because I am happy with modest means
I never asked the gods to make me rich.
But now, Poverty, I ask you to please
                        quit the scene.
Why this sudden, unprecedented request?
I want to see Zoilus hang himself.

My own

In your new, fashionable clothes, Zoilus,
                you sneer at mine,
                all threadbare.
Threadbare through and through, Zoilus,
                but my own.

Progress

I once saw a man hanging
for quite a while.
The posture improved his style.

Zoilus, who believes in progress,
should copy this.

Bullish enterprise

Castor, you're buying everything today.
You'll sell everything tomorrow.
Your money goes and grows a thousand ways.

Debt no debt

You're not in debt, Sextus. Never will be. No way.
A man is in debt only if he can pay.

Promises

Pollio, promises pour from you at night
when you've been drinking all evening.
You never keep a promise. Drink in the morning.

First thing

Not of yesterday's liquor my friend is reeking.
He drinks first thing in the morning.

Fraud

He's a fraud, prodding his gob with a toothpick.
He has no teeth.

Nothing left

You had four teeth left. A bad cough got rid of two.
Another fit and the other two were gone.
Laugh away to blazes now. There's nothing left
for a third fit of coughing to do.

Black and white

Molly's teeth are white, Dolly's black. How come?
Molly bought hers. Dolly's are her own.

Love

'Dick loves Tess.' 'Which Tess?' 'Tess with one eye.'
Tess wants one eye. Dick must want both.

Banishment

What I accuse others of
I'm guilty of, myself.

I'm guilty of myself.

No lie

She swears the hair she bought is her own.
Is she lying? No.

Age

If her years were as many
as the hairs of her head

she'd be three.

Hare

She sent me a hare and said,
'Eat this, you'll be handsome for a week.'
If she's telling the truth, it's clear
she never ate hare herself.

Without

I can do without your face, Chloe, and
without your neck, hands, eyes, legs, nose, shoulders.
Without going into detail, Chloe, I can do
without you altogether.

Passed off well

Atreus feasted Thyestes
on the bodies of his own sons.
Nobody complained.

What they see

Prattus is intensely stupid.
Most people see the intensity.
A few, the stupidity.

Miles

I'd like to spend days and nights with you, Joycus,
but there are two miles between us
and these two become four
since I have to walk back to my own place.
Quite often, you're not at home.
Often, when you are, you won't see visitors.
Often, too, you're interested only in your own recreation.

I don't mind walking two miles to see you
but I won't walk four miles not to see you.

Talkers

When these two talk in their usual way
the sun covers its face and turns away.

Masters

Maximus, I'm fishing for an invitation to your dinner.
You're fishing for somebody else's. We're fifty-fifty.
I hurry to attend your levée in the morning.
You're gone to attend somebody else's.
Fifty-fifty again.
I love to flatter you.
You love to flatter someone else.
Fifty-fifty yet again.
It's bad to be an arselicker's arselicker.

I think I'll be an onlooker.

Pepper

You used to send me a gift
of a pound of silver
but that pound has shrunk
to a half-pound of pepper.

My pepper is not that expensive, Sextus.

Moonscream

When Prattus makes what he thinks is love
the moon screams
and runs for cover.

Rich poverty

Rich people find anger a worthwhile investment.
Hatred costs less than giving presents.
Money manipulates feelings. That's its poverty.

Now

If you're a poor man now, Amos,
a poor man you'll remain.
Riches are given only
to rich men.

A choice of sources

Strutta has the biggest arse in Rome
and the smallest mind.
Which does she use
when ratting to, or about,
her own kind?

As a maker

As a maker of verse,
I have one abiding fear:
not being clear
to you.
Obscurity and confusion
I ansbacher as my own,
knowing they accumulate
while clarity goes out of date.

Cloak

Recently, Rufus, a man scrutinised me from head to toe.
When he'd completed his sly survey he said
'Are you really the great Martial whose jokes,
though occasionally obvious and not a little sick,
are known to everyone,
provided he hasn't the ear of a Dutchman?'
In a surge of modesty I admitted I was Martial.
'Then why is your cloak so threadbare?' he asked.
'Because I'm a bad poet' I replied.
(Who measures the pressure of the moon's blood?)

To prevent such a scene from happening again,
dear Rufus, please send me a respectable cloak
as soon as you can.
Let's show the world it's possible to be
a worthwhile poet and an elegant man.
Threadbare versifiers are not a pretty sight.
Dress them well. They may write less shite.

Yet

Rich? He sure is. Beyond dreams.
I can't stand him.
I hate that vain,
self-adoring bastard.

Yet, if he gave me
a grant or a huge prize
I'd write him a poem to bring
tears to his eyes.

Tireless

Africanus is a tireless legacy-hunter
though he's a wealthy man.
Fortune gives too much to many,
enough to none.

Birthdays

Clytus, you accumulate a vast amount of presents
by having eight birthdays a year.
The date is the first of every month
with the exception of three or four.
Your cheeks are smooth as polished marbles
washed up on the shore,
your hair blacker than the fallen mulberry
(what woman could ask for more?).
Yet to me you seem already old for who would
dream that Priam or Nestor
enjoyed as many birthdays as you?
Come off it, Clytus, quit your extortion,
if you persist in this trickery
and are not happy with one birthday a year
like all men in their rise and fall
I must conclude, dear Clytus, that you
were never born at all.

The real thing

Because you give fine presents
to widows and old men
you want me to call you
a generous man?

Your gifts are traps.

The killing hook is generous
to the greedy fish.
The crafty bait deceives
the eager game.
Let me tell you clearly
what true generosity is:

give a present to me.

December

It's December, presents are lunatics –
spoons, napkins, knives, writing-paper,
classy jars of delicious jam.
I've sent you nothing but my small books,
I must seem tight as a mackerel's arse
on a winter's night, and that's water-tight.
But I despise the treacherous generosity
of presents. Presents are like hooks,
the greedy fish is fooled by the fly he swallows.
In refusing to give presents to rich friends,
the poor man shows true generosity.

Martial the sinner

Prattus says my poems are sins. He
is right. I commit the sin of clarity
with unrelenting, lustful glee.
I see what I say, say what I see.
I love it when Prattus hates me.
He may be right, of course. For a moment, we agree.

Satisfaction

I wanted to give you a birthday present,
Quintus, but you wouldn't let me.
You're a strong man. Your words must be obeyed.
Let both sides of our situation be fulfilled.
   Send me a present, Quintus.
   That'll satisfy the pair of us.

Justice

There are times when only contradiction
does justice to a human. The word 'man'
hides, resides in 'woman'. The rest is 'wo'.
The god of words ordained it so.

All ears

More lies are told about truth
than are whispered in women's ears.
Many a name grows huge
when reduced to a whisper.

Boar

Garricus, when you swore by all that's holy
you'd make me an heir to a quarter
of your estate, I believed you
and sent you a flood of presents
including a spectacular Laurentian boar.
You invited senators and uppies to dinner
as a result of which many Romans look bilious,
with a taste of my boar in their mouths.

    Who will believe this?

I was not a guest, even at the bottom of the table,
I never received a rib or a bit of the tail,
I might as well be on a nameless Asian shore.
What hope have I of a quarter of your property
when I didn't receive a thousandth part
        of my own boar?

To be sure

He's chasing you for your money.
Will he honestly mourn your death?
If you want to be sure he will
leave him nothing.

To be honest

Money is filthy
yet I have always loved
whatever rhymes
with wealthy.

Recovery

The funeral pile was ready for the flames.
The crying wife was buying myrrh and cinnamon.
The grave, the coffin, the undertaker were ready.
In his will, Numa had made me his heir.
Then he got better.

Nothing

Whatever you ask for, Cinna, you say
      'Oh, it's nothing!'
Well, if it's nothing you ask for, Cinna,
      it's nothing I refuse.

True friend

You lent me five thousand pounds, Telessinus.
A great friend for getting me off the rack?
No, I'm the true friend. I paid it back.

When silence speaks

I've bought a place in the country, Cecil,
and am asking you for ten thousand pounds.
Your silence says 'You won't pay it back'.
That's why I'm asking for it, my friend.

Waiting for Cinna

When I ask you for money, Cinna,
give it, or refuse it.
You won't do either.
How long must I wait while you dither?
Ever heard of a straight answer?

What I want

I asked a friend to lend me a thousand pounds.
'You'll make plenty of money,' he said, 'if you study law.
Law is money, it's respectable, and it's nice.'
Give me what I want, my friend.
I don't want advice.

Half

Whoever gives Prattus half of what he asks for
will lose only that half.

Genius

My old friend Sextus knows how to refuse
not only when I ask him
but, in recent times,
before I ask him.
There's a certain bond between us.
I admire his mean, prophetic genius.

The point of praise

Listening to Selius laying the praise on thick
I hear him coming to dinner.
I hear his molars chewing my duck.

Original

He's original.
There's nothing he won't steal.
He mumbled once, 'I want it all!'
May one steal the impossible?

No doubt

He's your friend, he says. Of that there's no doubt.
He adores your roast boar, mullet, trout,
hare, chicken, sow's breast, oysters,
salmon and your famous wine.
If my dinners were as good as yours
he'd be a friend of mine.

Solitude

You invite three hundred people, all strangers to me.
When I'm invited and don't come, you express surprise,
you grumble, complain, grow truculent, start to wrangle.
I dislike dining in solitude, Fabullus.

Trier

Prattus tries to write. People say
words laugh at him and run away.
Most words hate to be led astray
though, if you're willing, they'll help you play.
Prattus tries to write. Olé! Olé!

Giving in

Teedeesus will say your towels are white as snow
though they stink of a season's filth.
When you comb what's left of your hair
he says you're gifted with the locks of Achilles.
If it's a hot day and you sweat profusely
he'll wipe the sweat from your forehead all day.
He'll praise you, admire you, flatter you until,
having suffered his endless attention,
        you give in
and say, 'Come to dinner, dear man,
and if you're running for the Senate
you have my Number One.'

For

What are words for, Dellabelle,
if not to make right actions possible?
You've heard me speak of love in Naples.

Revenge

I've discovered how to pay you back for not
inviting me to dinner, Lupercus. I'll get enraged,
you may invite me, entreat me, beg me to come
but I –

'Yes, what will you do?'you ask.
'What shall I do?' Hmmm... ...

Why, I shall come to dinner, kind Lupercus. I shall come.

Meaning

When one dines alone
one knows the meaning
of conversation.

Post-dinnerism

A favourite post-dinner moment of mine
is when I sip contradiction with wine.
How easily the human becomes divine.

No news is good news

You get invited to dinner because of your stories
which you make up endlessly, Gobgookus.
                You know
what's happening at court
the size of all the armies
the secrets of Government
the sources and fates of monies
the outcome before the battle's over
how many ships are on the sea
for whose tables Caesar's olives are growing.
                And you know
to whom the Lord of Heaven will offer favour.

Forget your fibby stories, Gobgookus.
Come to dinner this evening
but please, please,
don't tell me any news.

The art of quelling

You like dining out, Cantankerus,
though you're a loud, abusive bully.
Quell your hideous temper, if you're able.
Don't be gluttonous and vicious at once
at anybody's table.
You may stuff yourself like a starving slave
but try to behave.

Knowing Shrudus

You invite me, Shrudus, when you know
I've asked some friends to come.
Please excuse me. I dine at home.

Lifelong companion

Everyone in Rome knows
Rud was born in the Province of Hate
and takes It with him
      wherever he goes.

Sloucher

Prattus slouches the streets, looking
for things and people to hate.
He is an unfinished sentence
nobody should bother to punctuate.

The beauty of worry

Trouble-free, Sippus, you are intolerable.
When you're worried, you're delightful.
Trouble-free, you're surly and ignorant,
you spit contempt at everyone,
you treat no one as a human being.
When you're worried, you're generous,
your demeanour is respectful,
you invite people to dinner.
Be worried, Sippus.

Two souls

I know two souls
who always go to bed late
fearing their sleep
may lessen their hate.

A civilised man

Pappus, they say your wine is not good,
it made you a widower four times.
I don't believe that. You're a civilised man.
Nevertheless, my thirst is suddenly gone.

Staying put

Scrungus says he never dines at home.
That's true. Eats nothing, stays put
when nobody asks him out.

Perfection

Cecil won't dine without a wild boar:
his perfect companion at dinner.

To a man of words

You say you don't like dining out, Classicus.
You're lying.
If you don't like dining out, why do you go?
'I am under an obligation to do so,' you say.
True. So is Selius.
Come off it, Classicus. A friend asks you to dinner.
You're a man of words. There's yes. There's no.
Don't go.

Smack

What will they say of me in the future?
His words smack of human nature.

Lot

Prattus stinks, therefore he is.
Prattus thinks, therefore he's not.
Non-thoughts, foul odours
arc his mortal lot.

Best

My best poem will be one line,
define the void, celebrate oblivion.
I shall write it after a perfect dinner
and many glasses of my favourite wine.

Subtlety

Rud is a subtle bastard.
    I'm so obvious at times
    I rob myself of breath.
Rud should be tied to a goat's arse
    and scuttered to death.

Not yet

I pray the God who's not born yet.
'Please help me (having heard her) to forget!'

Progress

My friend Pudens is marrying Claudia.
May their marriage be forever blessed.
They are perfectly suited to each other
like the elm and the tender vine
    the lotus and the water
    the myrtle and the shore
    Athenian honey and Massic wine.
May Claudia love Pudens when he's old,
may she seem young and beautiful in his eyes
when youth is far behind her.
May their marriage be a calm progress
towards ever deepening happiness.
When they lie down at night, may darkness bless
    togetherness.

Repetition

He ignored his father once.
Now he's bypassed by his sons
following their own stars.
Their sons will follow theirs.
I study the fertile, callous years.

Friends

Lycoris, in her tantrum-throwing life,
has buried all her female friends.
I wish she would be friendly with my wife.

I might

Phil wants to marry me but I won't marry Phil.
She's such an old stinker, a bitter old pill.
I might marry her, though, if she were older still.
If we both reach a hundred, I certainly will.

Wise folk

Phil, you want to marry Priscus.
It doen't surprise me. Not many women
are wise as you.
Priscus, however, has no wish to marry.
He's wise too.

Partners

Fabius buries his wives; Christilla, her husbands.
Each waves the funeral torch over the marriage bed.
Dear Venus, arrange that this pair be engaged.
One coffin will be enough to contain the dead.

Source

Gemellus is keen to marry Maronilla.
He is ardent, persistent, gentle, generous.
Is she so beautiful, then?
No, she's hideous.
One look is enough to put anyone off.
What, then, is the source of her charm?
Her consumptive cough.

Rare weather

The most glorious weather is, will be,
when two souls shine together,
brighter than the summer sea.

Honest woman

On each of the tombs of her seven husbands
Chloe placed the inscription 'The work of Chloe'.
A hard worker and an honest woman
whichever way you look at her.
Be careful how and when you do.
You may be the work of Chloe, too.

Harvest

This is the seventh wife you've buried
in your field, Philero.
No one gets a more fruitful return from his field
than you do.
Many a rich farmer would weep,
watching the harvest you reap.

Prattus and heaven

Had Prattus the heavens' embroidered cloths
he'd wipe his arse with them.

A geography

Birds of the air know
the man with a house everywhere
has a home nowhere.

Poetry

If Martial's truth were told
all that I give
is less than I withhold.

Living

When I remember
success, failure,
friend, enemy,
wife, lover

I live twice over.

Crafty Bassus

Past the Porta Capena, leaking as usual;
past the spot where the priests of Cybele
wash their equipment in the river Almo;
past the field holy with the memory of the Horatii;
past the Temple of Hercules the Tiny
packed with worshippers,

       Bassus drives in his coach
carrying cabbages with bulging heads,
leeks, lettuces, beetroots, carrots, turnips,
hares and a sucking-pig.

The footman runs, carrying eggs wrapped in hay.

Is Bassus on his way to Rome?

Not on your nanny. Crafty Bassus is headed
for his Big House in the country.

The curse

The curse of poverty is that its grip
makes the poor believe there's no escape.

Measurement

Mean? He wouldn't give
a starving child
the steam off his piss.

Not on honeymoon

When you fuck, you shit.
Honeymooners don't do that.
They wait.
There's a slime and a pace for everything.

Settling down

Back from the honeymoon
and rose-petals on the bed
she settles down
with the meanest prick she ever met.

Strolling through riches

Mamurra spends hours strolling through the Square
where wealthy Rome displays its riches.
He looks at tables, fiddles with the covers,
asks to look at hanging works of ivory,
measures a settee inlaid with tortoise-shell,
is clearly sad it's too small for his dining-table.
He applies his nose to see if bronzes have the right
Corinthian smell; finds fault with statues;
complains of common glass in crystal vases
and sets aside ten agate jars for himself,
tests the weight of cups and antique goblets,
counts the jewels that jingle in girls' earrings,
seeks real sardonyxes at every counter
and makes an offer for some large jaspers.
Finally, as he leaves at five in the afternoon,
he buys two mugs for a penny
and takes them home. Tonight, Mamurra
will be an expert on the riches of Rome.

At my door

You ask me why is it
you always arrive at my door
panting and late?

Lose weight.

Youth

Polla, why send me fresh flowers?
Send me old roses. Yours. Only yours.
Youth is more than a matter of years.

Learning time

Master, let your students experience the sun.
No cane, stick, leather. No young hands burning.
In summer, healthy boys are fit for learning.

Failing

His goodwill towards me is steadily failing
but I keep on calling.
Would he see me if my
goodwill towards him began to die?

Inspiration

I heard a Roman intellectual say
forms of poverty can be an inspiration.
Would he think the same after three days
begging for bread
on an empty stomach, a despised head?

Too late

Glory arrives too late
if it comes only to one's ashes.
There's much to be said for celebrating
until darkness kneels to morning.

A happy life

What constitutes a happy life?
Enough money to meet your needs
steady work
a comfortable fire
a clear distance from law
a minimum of city business
a peaceful mind and a healthy body
simple wisdom and firm friends
enjoyable dinners and plain living
nights free from care
a virtuous wife who's not a prude
enough sleep to make the darkness short
contentment with the life you have,
avoiding the sneer, the poisoned sigh;
no fear of death
and no desire to die.

Retiring impulse

After a bracing walk and a swim
he said to his loved one,
'I think I'll apply for a Disability Pension.'
He did, got it. He's training for the Marathon.

Translation

Why do Martialites bother to translate?
I chuckle (especially if it's good)
at the many ways I'm misunderstood
and I realise, when some poems ring true,
they spring from me misunderstanding you.

Busy body

At every gathering in town
he's so busy licking arses
his grey verse is turning brown.

Taste

I taste what the ageing blood remembers.
      I live my days
unencumbered by numbers.
      I respect true praise.

Assault

When my wife assaults me
      with the inside of her head
the inside of mine becomes a recently
      vacated hospital bed.

Early

The whore is out early. Not yet noon.
So early. Beautiful. Prowling for men
who're not yet
prowling for her.
Fair play to the early riser.

High Art

Integrity is the name of the game.
The more intrepid you are, the blacker your fame.
O hang the old devil, what's in a name?

Future births

I have my bad words, too, but I don't fret.
I dream of words not born yet.
The future tells me what to forget.

You in me in you

Remember, friend (yes, you are my friend
and Rome knows this is true),
as you work hard translating me
I am translating you.

My joy

I thought, once, when I closed the book at night
all the words would run mocking and sneering.
I slept and woke and slept and woke again.
Imagine my joy when I opened the book in the morning.

His own

When a man comes into his own
God knows what he leaves behind
or what he's about to face
in time not yet into mind.

Daisies

I talk in her sleep, she talks in mine.
We're fresher than daisies in the morning.

One wild night

In the course of one wild night in Malahide
he lived his Odyssey and his Iliad.
All his gods inhabited his head,
his heart's blood poured gratitude to the dead
who gave him words he'd never known before
where the sea caressed and threatened the shore.

Clarity

'If he gossips to me
about you
he'll gossip to you
about me.'

So

Like any man of flesh and bone
So Rome of gossip and stone.

Reasons

Your penis is withered
        your arse is itchy,
two good reasons
        you're such a bitchy
bastard night and day.
Be like your penis. Wither away.

Offer

Marry you, Galla? Never.
        Among the snooty bunch
my penis is busy
        between breakfast and lunch.

There's a pair of us in it

Your life is a lie.
I believe you.

You spew your bilious verse.
I praise you.

You sing like a starving crow.
I adore you.

You get pissed.
I get footless.

You fart and stink the house.
I say I'm sorry.

You screw around, cheating your wife.
I know fuck-all about that.

You never give me a penny.
I sigh with gratitude.

You promise to leave me a fortune.
You're one magnanimous man.

Please die as soon as you.

Steam

Will she sleep with me
        or not?
How can I tell what's steaming
        in the pot?
She plays it cool. I like it hot.

Dignity

She bears her sad secret with dignity.
Would she say the same of me?
If I heard her, would I agree?
Secrets are Supreme Court company.

Remember

When you feel you're the top man in the land
Remember the acid dwarf, knife in hand.

A pity

Swans sing before they die,
     the bells of heaven ring.
A pity Crowsus didn't die
     before he learned to sing.

Day and night

We get on OK during daylight hours.
Midnight sees the full brunt of her powers.
She'd bring an empire to its knees
and open up unconquered countries.

Martial on Martial

Catullus is a solemn bloke.
Martial finds philosophy in a joke
and smiles when he sees lightning strike
the water first, and then the rock.

No touch

I know you're bright, beautiful and rich.
Why have I no desire to touch?
Entranced I may be, but out of reach.

How to cope

You are completely bewitched. Your first time.
Well, be bewitched. But get out of Rome.

Immorality

'Your poems, Martial, are immoral mavericks.'
'I'm glad my poems give you a pain in the ethics.'

Neelus

'A poem is a lie, Martial. A lie is a world of its own.'
'Thank you, Neelus. Is that your first epigram?'

Competition

Thought of a star makes a star of thought.
Poets compete. Poems do not.

Substitution

Grey hair dyed black, we all know that.
But can you substitute slim for fat?

The cost of things

You shit in a golden urn
that looks divine.
We drink together. Your shit
is more expensive than your wine.

New knowledge

The stars are grieving
        and the gods are gone.

Grabitus knows money
        is your only man.

Playing

She's playing shy while showing off.
Her delicate glance says she likes it rough.
Sensitive distaste can never get enough.

New Year

Last year you always answered 'yes'.
'No' is the measure of your current prowess.

New life

Because she messed with the gods
she was turned into a rock
and her tears became a waterfall.
When children climb all over her
their delight enters her soul.

Late

He sits up late in a cold, dark place.
Why? His wife's face.

Treasures

I wrote to her. No reply. Not a word. Her friend
read the letter. Strange how treasures are found.

Chewers

Self-hatred is a creepy killer,
self-importance a strutting joker.
At dinner, sometimes, I sit and watch them
chewing each other.

Menu

When Grabitus tells Rome
what he had for dinner
he never mentions
poisonous chatter.
For every sewer rat
there's a sure-tongued ratter.

For the first time

'I love Latin,' she said. 'When I read Martial
I understood, for the first time,
my twenty-first century world
of war, famine, boredom, haste, drugs,
murder, hate, greed, stink, money,
slavery, torture, stress, mindlessness,
corruption and crime.

Two thousand years on, how is Rome?'

Almost

The day's work is done
the night's drinking over.
In recent years, he's almost
glad that at such times
he has no lover.

Passion and permanence

What he, in love, bedwhispers to her
is printed on air, scrawled on water.

A minute

So what if I write all day? All night?
There are those who'll say
'It's obvious, isn't it,
he wrote the damned thing in a minute?'
Maybe they're right. Small things
remind me how a blackbird sings.

Lelia's solution

Kiss my hand or my lips? Think. Which is worse?
If you can't make up your mind, dear, kiss my arse.

The makers

God made the country
Man made the town
The Devil made the small
spiteful places

in between.

Art and life

Why spend money on Mona Lisa
            hanging on a wall
when you can have Molly Polly Fox
            for nothing at all?

Another page

Did it happen or not happen, as they say?
Happiness is another page away.

Sanity

is a matter of touch and go.
It depends on making sure
there are certain things
you'll never know.

Let the Roman sun blind whom it will

and the North Pole guess
what's hidden under snow.

A word

I am nine years older than Christ.
Why did we never meet?
Rome could do with a word of love
in every street.

Another

Another war, sick children starving,
       cities burning,
    men incapable of learning,
cruel song at the century's turning.

In a chair

Is there anything as mad
as the mind of a man
sitting in a chair
alone in a room
bombing everywhere?

In my time

I've licked arses in my time,
turned stinking fact into perfumed fable.
If a poet plods with empty pockets
he won't put bread on the table.

That's me

If you hear sharp midnight cries
that's mc, shooting folly as it flies.

Education

I have my enemies. I love to look
into their eyes.
I have my friends. I love to see
their eyes look into mine.

Seeing through, being seen through:
my favourite education.

Young lover

He learned to love, to fail and weep
and to accept
eternal sleep.

Chained

I saw a man chained to a rock,
a vulture eating his liver.

'Would you,' I asked, 'change your mind
if you were set free?'

'Never.'

Strange

Strange thing, loneliness.
How it comes and goes
like poison at a dinner-table
or the smell of a rose.

Skills

Certain people, grown tired of killing,
learn the skills of ruling
those who condemned them once.
Some governments are built on dead bones.

Prayer

What prayer would I say
to this new God
spoken of at home and abroad?

May you make us all
less stupid.

Perfection

Lecherous hosts yearn
for your presence at dinner.

Are you the perfect dish, done to a turn?

Never again

Krockus swears he'll never go
to a brothel again.

Why does he go home?

Quest

My days and nights are a quest for brevity.
Why?

Fun

He dresses as a woman, now and then,
and will tell you, with unkempt delight,
what it's like to be a bride for a night
      and why it's fun
        to be a man again.

The vainest

Of all vain men (sharp readers know it)
the vainest is a lazy poet.
He may know how, but will not do it.

Too deeply

The best poet I know is blind.
He sees too deeply into humankind.

Agreement

You say my poems are ugly. I agree.
You are what I see.

Wild teachers

Strange how wild sky-creatures teach.
Swallows starlings seagulls fly
with such abandon I believe
they were born to search the sky
for a nest of love
always out of reach.

Martial law

When Martial law comes into force
clarity claps hands with verse,
guides the woman through her trance
and knows the dancer from the dance.

Sign

I walk the streets of Rome
        looking for a sign
of what I most desire –
        one true line.
This life would be well spent
        if such were mine.

Trial

The lawyer confronts the poet in court.
After ten hours of questioning,
        the lawyer wins.
The poet cries a little, then laughs and laughs
        and laughs
and finds a warm, improper spot
        to celebrate his sins.

Meeting

When law and justice meet in the light
each wonders who the other is.

The art of war

Soldiers never afraid to risk their lives
are quivering cowards before their wives.

Cold power

This icy bitch chops coward and hero.
When she slides into a hot bath
the temperature sinks below zero.

Learning

This cat claws hard to hide its shit.
You claw, but not to bury yours.
Look at the creature and learn that
a cat may teach the cutest hoors.

Wall

Mind what you say
near a wall.
Never know who's behind.

Gratitude

It was a most gentle kiss. Yes. Truly.
Yes. A most gentle kiss.
And the giver is miles away, walking
    in soft April rain.
    I am alone again.
Not that I object, mind you. I am
    a grateful man.

My wish, my work

Good luck to the busy living
and the peaceful dead.
I write for bread.

Warning

Warn the Army. The danger's real.
Blowjob Biddy is on the prowl.
Grabitus loves to see her kneel.

Today

Today, Grabitus is eighty-five
How long do maggots live?

Out

As I slip my key in her lock
        this icy night
I know what it means
        to be locked out.

Enough

He doesn't need a wife.
His sister is enough.

I hear myself

Transfixed by stars this icy night
        I hear myself say
'Why do the most beautiful buildings in Rome
        get in my way?'

A long time

Read Copycat as much as you like
in bad and fair weather.
You'll walk a long time behind a duck
before you pick up an eagle's feather.

Twice

A wife will be twice as loving
if her chain is to her liking.

I watch a man design a chain.
Who'll be shackled? Not that man.

Tickling

That man who knows how to tickle his bum
laughs when the mood takes him.

Time to go

Towards the end of the week
the fish and the guest start to rot.
Throw them out.

Expert

He talks, talks. I listen, listen. I rise, crawl
away from the man who knows it all.

What she means

When I see Apuleius on his golden ass
I understand the needs of my favourite goddess
and what she means when she speaks of Paradise.

Leaders

Blind runners always run in Rome
with a guide who can see
but who is leading whom
is never clear to me.

Age

Her age? Painted, jewelled, she's twenty-one.
At night, deconstructed, she's forty-nine.
Come morning, age is what she decides on.
Time is her servant, most of the time.

Still wondering

I escaped from Spain and came to Rome.
I'm still wondering, where is home?

At school

I study Lesbia's pet sparrow
pranking on my window-sill.
This bird knows much about love.
I'm back at school.

A question of feathering

This Roman poet loves to walk about, looking
sensitive and solemn. True style, he says, true style.

If Lesbia's pet sparrow feathered his balls
would he smile?

Drifters

It tortured me in darkness. I wrote it down.
There. Whatever it is, I suppose it's my own
though it may drift away into another person.
Poems are drifters. A mind is an ocean.

Drink

A word is a drop of blood.
Drink the word. Fortitude.
Drink the word again. Blood.

Summit

I climbed Parnassus once or twice
and found the summit an icy spot,
so back with me to the Age of Gold,
a Roman laneway, in bed with Millie,
happy bodies heavenly hot.
Parnassians are not a loving lot
except for one I'll never forget.

Prayer

Here is my prayer.
May peace, health and wealth prevail
and I enjoy the company of friends.
War is for devils. To hell with war!

Gone

So many roads to travel. One end.
'I hear he's gone,' says his best friend.

Inventors

Who invented the joke?

Some dry shyster caught out in the rain?
Some yapper mouthing his way out of trouble?
Some gossip developing a new technique?
Someone in pain?
Some poet afraid to question?

Gift of the years

Over the years, Grabitus has found
it's hard to fool an enemy,
easy to cheat a friend.
Grabitus chooses the easy way.

Little poems

Martial, she said, your little poems will never do.
I know a graveyard with more fame than you.

The night

You say I'm widely loathed
for the poems I write.
If, as you say, you cannot sleep
how do you spend the night?

Abyss

The old Queen longs to be fucked by a bull.
What commoner knows
what it's like to be Royal?

Easy

She's had her fill of complex knackers.
Tonight, she needs easy pleasure
        to sweeten her ears
                and cream her knickers.

A tiny bird

Of all the creatures human and inhuman
I know in Rome
Lesbia's pet sparrow is the most relaxed,
happy and at home.

Why should this be so? A tiny bird,
composed and modest in its ways,
perches on her lady's shoulder,
star of all the days.

Time to fling

What chokes a soaring imagination?
Good behaviour turning to inhibition.
A kind of killing sophistication.

Time to fling the whole lot off
and jump in the sea, thrilling and rough.

Whenever

Whenever I say a prayer
I know why birds' wings
are loved by the air.

Ludicus

He sleeps all day, works and pleasures all night,
the right man to spread an Empire's might.

One day, in disrepute, he'll kill himself. Later,
Rome will hear how he died at his leisure.

Face to face

She tells me why she had to put him away.
As she speaks I look at her,
trying to understand. I come face to face
with the darkness of a flower,
the calm aftermath of a fever.

Only the best

'You're the most shameless bloody liar,' she said,
        'from Rome to Portmagee.
You may tell your lies to any knacker you like
        but please keep the best lies for me.'

Walker

When she walks the streets of Rome
she drives some men out of their wits,
her arse rippling like a bag of ferrets
or a pair of duckeggs in a silk hankie.

Only answer

'Have I hurt others? Did I almost kill?
My only answer is a sleeping pill.'

Charge

She swears she was raped by Sam the thief.
Sam says this charge is just beyond belief.

The stroller

Prattus asks, seeing Martial stroll through town,
'Is this clown a poet? Is this poet a clown?'
Knowing how Prattus hates a shred of doubt
I let him ponder, figure the stroller out.

Arrangement

Arrange for Cullus to get a prize.
No matter what you write
you have his slavish praise.

Follow the formula

In Rome, you won't be forgiven
if you write
a challenging poem.

Be sensitive and bland.
Join the self-elected band.

Another reminder

A gobsmacking city spit
is interestingly black.

Reminds me of how some poets
        love
to stab in the back.

When they meet

This poet fills his life with poison
    and makes his poetry beautiful.
This other has a beautiful life
    and makes his poetry poisonful.

When they meet they stop and smile,
agree it's all a matter of style.
Style, they say, is the name of the living game.
They part then, go their ways. Different? Or the same?

Look

Walk with me. Look. Are the gods here? Or gone?
If I change your mind, I will change creation.

Educating faces

Walking the streets, I see faces
that educate me in the matter of Rome:

a rich man is at home in strange places,
a poor man is a stranger at home.

Certain parts

On certain parts of Rome
money falls like rain.
I walk a different street, meet
        begging women, cowed hungry children.
        I want to turn pain
        into bread and wine.

Caesar

She holds out a cup. Her eyes are sick.
I rifle myself for a coin. Caesar.
Nothing doing. Out of here. Quick.

Fearing freedom

The dead have a freedom
the living are afraid of.
Make love on a hill-top,
in a black pit make love.
The dead have a freedom
the living are afraid of.

It may be

Rome wasn't built in a day
but if some have their way
it may be destroyed in a night.

The way

The way we treat our dead
is a sure guide
to heart and head.

No

No, I don't write poems to serve a cause
unless it be when they
cause joy to flood your eyes.

A poet's teeth

When a poet's teeth begin to rot
and he becomes what he believes he's not,
the problem of identity slips away
like an old wasp hiding where it may.
Parnassus is a bed of well-saved hay.
The old wasp pulls in its wings and falls asleep
while tired shadows down the mountain creep.

My own

Why won't I marry a rich woman?
Because I don't want to be known

as my wife's husband. Whatever my identity is,
I'd like it to be my own.

Two

I got two strong smells today.
A woman smelled of fish,
a man of money.

The fish is fresher company.
I'm hooked.

The thought

Prattus never flushes the toilet.
Some sensitive bastards
can't bear the thought
of parting with their shit.

Judges

He said, over his umpteenth glass of wine,
'I can't sleep any longer, no matter
how much I drink.
Memories terrorise every bone.
Darkness and silence are merciless judges.'

Lives

How many of my friends lead lives
they truly wish to lead?
Do I? Who dares live for himself?
Why are the days flying past, vanishing,
lost to us, discarded, betrayed, accusing us?
Something fears that calm, free, adventurous thing.
Some crucial voice has ceased to sing.
It is time to return to the true life –
good talk, good books, shaded spots,
hot baths, the Virgin's spring.
I'm ready. Are you coming?
The world is opening. Are you coming?

Day and night

By day, Lucy is all right
but come the night, I want Mirabel,
sweet expert in the business of delight.
Lucy grounds me.
Mirabel is flight.

Readers

I have my readers. I never mind
being misunderstood if misunderstanding
lets a reader see something
I know nothing of
but am glad to hear about.
A reader's eyes are not my eyes
and what I say may not be what is seen.
I say green, he sees blue.
I say blue, she sees green.
Eyes are gifted, adventurous things.
New worlds open when a poem sings.

Coldest moment

His coldest moment came when,
as a result of nothing
but the callous, boring
evidence of the years,
he lost his belief
in belief.

The right kind

I aspire to the right kind of madness.
What is that?
Whatever tells me again and again,
I'm close to being rain

    and will pour down
        on Rome
    long after I'm gone.

Plodder

When I plod into my cell of words
and turn the key

something I have no name for
is free.

May the sun that is the king of light
bring health and happiness to all who work
on land and sea

and may the moon that is the lamp of the poor
shine
on what I know of me.